Sweet Potato Cook

All Types of Sweet Potato Recipes You Can Try at Home!

By: Logan King

Copyright © 2021 by Logan King

Edition Notice

The author has taken any step to make sure this book is accurate and safe. Every info is checked. However, every step you take following the book do it with caution and on your own accord.

If you end up with a copied and illegal version of this book please delete it and get the original. This will support the author to create even better books for everyone. Also, if possible report where you have found the illegal version.

This book is under copyright license which means no one is allowed to make any changes, prints, copies, republish or sell it except for the author.

Table of Contents

Introduction

We often lack adequate time to make delicious meals at home and end up consuming already prepared meals from eateries. Well, that shouldn't be the case always because you can always spare some moment and make quality meals at your home. Are you having plenty of sweet potatoes at your home? Well, don't let them go bad or prepare the same recipes repeatedly because this cookbook is authentic.

What is more, is that you can use different cooking appliances to make these recipes. If you have an oven or an air fryer, you can make sweet potato chips, sweet potato fries, baked casseroles with sweet potatoes with a nice and tender texture. You can as well make sweet potato stews over the stove and serve them with other accompaniments. Once you go through all the recipes in this cookbook, you will realize you have plenty of ideas to transform meals at your home.

You don't need to spend the entire day in the kitchen to make these meals. As a busy person, you can spare a few minutes and fix one of the recipes during the day. Again, you can use your off days when not quite busy to prepare the recipes that require more time. The good news is that you can prepare most of these meals in plenty and reserve some for later use.

Start gradually, and with time, you will master the art of making different meals using sweet potatoes.

More Information related to Sweet Potatoes

Sweet potatoes are available worldwide, and any person from kids to adults can consume meals made with sweet potatoes. They make wholesome and tasty vegan, vegetarian, and other meals made with meat.

Sweet potatoes have a wide range of minerals and other nutrients that help us in our daily lives. Besides nourishing our bodies, sweet potatoes also keep a person satisfied for hours after consumption. They aren't limited to any person or any function. You can make a snack and serve them at a birthday party or for any other function.

While making sweet potatoes, common spices such as nutmeg, cinnamon, ground cloves, cayenne pepper, dried basil, among many others, bring good flavors and taste. Sweet potato soups are the best accompaniments during cold weather days. Explore the recipes in this cookbook and realize the value of sweet potatoes in our lives.

Sweet Potato and Lentil Soup

Little can go wrong with this hearty, healthy, and vegetarian-friendly delicacy. You will savor the rich taste in no time with the present company.

Serving Size: 6

Cooking Time: 15 minutes

Ingredients:

- 1 tbsp, vegetable oil
- 1 white onion, diced
- ½ cup chopped carrots
- 2 cups cubed sweet potatoes
- ½ cup chopped celery
- 6 cups vegetable broth
- 2 cups diced tomatoes
- 1 cup lentils
- 1 tsp of dried rosemary
- 1 tsp of dried thyme
- Salt
- Pepper

Instructions:

On a stove set at medium-high temperature, heat the oil in a large saucepan.

Sauté the onion, carrots, sweet potatoes, and celery for around five minutes. Add the broth, tomatoes, lentils, rosemary, and thyme.

Bring to a boil, then reduce heat.

Simmer while covered until the flavors meld and all the ingredients are cooked through and tender.

Add salt and Pepper to taste and serve.

Roasted Sweet Potato Salad

This simple and easy-to-prepare roasted sweet potato salad provides an excellent way of using leftover roasted potatoes from previous meals. Take advantage of your favorite salad dressing to give the salad an extra kick.

Serving Size: 4

Preparation Time: 5 minutes

Ingredients:

- ½ cup chopped pecans
- 2 cups roasted sweet potatoes
- 1 cup halved grape tomatoes
- 3 cups baby spinach
- 1 sliced red onion
- ½ cup salad dressing

Instructions:

Add and combine the pecans, sweet potatoes, tomatoes, baby spinach, and onion in a bowl.

Add your preferred salad dressing, toss to coat, and serve.

Gouda Mixed Sweet Potato Mash

The Gouda Mixed Sweet Potato Mash is an incredible and cheesy delicacy that you will enjoy with your family. So why wait to satisfy the craving in the future when you can quickly fix this dish today? You will thank me later!

Serving Size: 12

Cooking Time: 35 minutes

Ingredients:

- 6 cubed Yukon gold potatoes
- 2 cubed sweet potatoes
- ½ cup 2% milk
- ¼ tsp pepper
- 1 tsp paprika
- 1 cup shredded gouda cheese
- 1/2 tsp salt

Instructions:

In a large pan, place the Yukon Gold and sweet potatoes in. Put it into a Dutch oven and bring the water to cover the ingredients. Let it sit to boil before lowering the heat.

Cook it (uncovered) for 10 to 15 minutes till tender. Drain the contents and mash the sweet potatoes as you mix in the milk gradually. Add pepper, paprika, cheese, and salt to taste.

Serve and enjoy.

Sweet Potato Salad with Black Beans and Pepper

This is a healthy and hearty dish to enjoy with present company. You will not only enjoy the rich flavor, but the freshness the salad gives it. What's more? You can always fix it in less than an hour.

Serving Size: 10

Cooking Time: 10 minutes

Ingredients:

- 15 oz. rinsed and drained black beans
- 1 cup chopped fresh cilantro
- 1 garlic clove
- 1 chopped jalapeno pepper
- 1 diced red bell pepper
- 1 chopped red onion
- 1½ lbs. cubed sweet potatoes
- 1/2 cup olive oil (divided)
- 2 juiced limes
- Salt as needed
- Black Pepper to taste

Instructions:

Slice the sweet potatoes, onions, and red bell pepper into a bowl.

Separately, drizzle a tbsp of olive oil into a cookie sheet.

Place the veggies on the sheet and cook for 10 minutes at 400°F till soft. Mix properly till smooth and remove it to fully cool.

Drain the water and rinse the beans.

In a bowl, mix the beans, salt, black pepper, and the veggies properly before pouring it over the salad.

Sprinkle with the fresh lime juice and serve.

Apple and Sweet Potato Quinoa

Quinoa redefined! The apple and sweet potato quinoa give you the perfect filling meal to win your family and friends over. It has an incredibly rich taste, and what's more? You can easily fix it when running out of time.

Serving Size: 6

Cooking Time: 30 minutes

Ingredients:

- 2¼ cups chicken or vegetable stock
- 1 cup rinsed quinoa
- 2 tbsp canola oil
- 3 cubed sweet potatoes
- 2 chopped shallots
- 3 sliced apple
- 1/2 cup additional stock or white wine
- 1/2 tsp salt
- 2 cups rinsed and drained black beans

Instructions:

In a large pot with some water, put the stock and quinoa and bring it to a boil.

Put the heat to low, cover, and let it simmer for 20 minutes. Turn off the stove when the liquid nearly absorbs.

Meanwhile, take a 6 or 8 quarts stock pot, put in oil, and heat it on medium heat.

Add the sweet potatoes and shallots and stir properly. Let it cook for 5 minutes.

Into the mix, add the sliced apples and let it cook for a further 8 minutes to make the potatoes and apples tender.

Add the wine and salt and stir properly as you boil the mixture uncovered. Cook for a minute or till the wine evaporates.

Into the mixture, add the black beans and quinoa. Heat further till properly cooked before serving.

Sweet Potato Nachos

Sweet Potato Nachos is the perfect movie night snack pick for you and friends or family. This cheesy snack contains vegetables. You can satiate your cheesy craving while keeping your calories down. What's more? You only need under an hour to prepare it for your enjoyment.

Serving Size: 4

Cooking Time: 55 minutes

Ingredients:

- 2 sliced sweet potatoes
- 1 tbsp. olive oil
- 1 minced garlic clove
- 1 tsp paprika
- Black pepper to taste
- 1 tsp salt
- 1 cup drained black beans
- ¼ cup chopped spring onions
- 1 cup grated cheddar cheese

Instructions:

Put the oven settings to preheat at 425°F and line a baking sheet with parchment paper and arrange in the sliced potatoes. Drizzle the potatoes with olive oil to achieve an even coating.

In a bowl, mix the minced garlic, paprika, and pepper.

Mix in salt before dusting the mixture over the potatoes.

Put the potatoes into your oven and bake for two periods of 20 minutes each. Ensure you turn the potatoes after the first baking period.

Transfer the baked potatoes into a skillet and sprinkle it with black beans and onions. Top it off with cheese.

Return the topped potatoes into the oven for another 5 minutes to melt the cheese.

Serve hot and enjoy.

Pumpkin and Sweet Potato Pilau

For all the vegetable lovers out there, this meal ranks as a must-try. It is tasty, nutritious, and will give you the necessary energy or kick to sustain your busy day.

Serving Size: 8

Cooking Time: 1 hour 40 minutes

Ingredients:

- 2 tbsp olive oil
- 2 cups cubed sweet potato
- 2 cups cubed pumpkin
- 1 tbsp minced garlic
- 1 diced yellow onion
- 1 cup brown rice
- 4 cups vegetable broth
- ½ tsp pepper
- ½ tsp salt

Instructions:

Preheat your oven to 400°

Meanwhile, arrange the sweet potato and pumpkin in a single file or layer on an oiled or greased sheet pan. Bake it for 40 minutes till tender.

Remove the baked sweet potato and pumpkin layer from the oven and set it aside.

Pour the oil into a skillet and heat at medium temperature. Add the garlic and onion and sauté till the onions are soft.

Into the frying onion mixture, add rice, broth, pepper, and salt.

Have the mixture boil, then reduce the heat. Cover the skillet and let it simmer for 45 minutes.

Add the sweet potato and pumpkin pieces and stir well.

Roasted Sweet Potato and Prosciutto Salad

Noting can beat the iconic blend of prosciutto and sweet potato. This wholesome meal is nutritious and perfect for you and your family.

Serving Size: 8

Cooking Time: 1 hour 15 minutes

Ingredients:

- 4 tbsp olive oil
- 3 cubed medium sweet potatoes
- 1/2 tsp divided salt
- 1/8 tsp pepper
- 1/2 cup thinly sliced prosciutto
- 1/4 cup chopped sweet red pepper
- 1/2 cup sliced radishes
- 1/3 cup sliced and toasted pecans
- 2 sliced green onions, divided
- 1 tbsp lemon juice
- 1 tsp honey

Instructions:

Preheat your oven to 400° Into a large and greased baking pan, put in your sweet potatoes. Sprinkle half of the oil and salt over the sweet potatoes. Add the pepper and toss the mixture properly as it roasts.

Sprinkle a little of the prosciutto over the mixture and continue roasting for 15 minutes (ensure the prosciutto turns crispy, and the sweet potatoes become tender.

Into a large bowl, transfer the blend and let it sit to cool down a bit. Add the red pepper, radishes, pecans, and half of the onions. After this, use a small bowl to mix the remaining oil, salt, lemon juice, and honey. Mix properly to obtain a fine blend and drizzle the mixture atop the salad. Toss the salad to mix and sprinkle the rest of the green onions.

Caramelized Sweet Potato Veggies with White-Wine Vinegar

Enjoy the taste explosion of your life with the caramelized sweet potato veggies with white-wine vinegar. The meal is not only delicious but simple to fix. What's more? You can quickly cook the meal for you and present company.

Serving Size: 4

Cooking Time: 25 minutes

Ingredients:

- 2 tbsp olive oil
- 1 red onion, quartered
- 2 sweet potatoes, cubed
- Black pepper to taste
- Salt as needed
- 10 oz. thawed cut green beans
- 1/3 cup walnuts
- 1 cup plain low-fat yogurt
- 1 crushed garlic clove
- 2 tbsp white wine vinegar
- 10 oz. chopped red-leaf lettuce

Instructions:

Preheat the oven to 450°

In a large baking sheet, put in oil, onions and the sweet potatoes. Add pepper and salt and roast till the sweet potatoes become tender.

Mix the green beans and the walnuts and cook for 5 minutes till tender.

In a small bowl, add the yogurt, garlic, and vinegar to mix. Add pepper and salt to taste.

Garnish the lettuce with the vegetable mixture.

Pour with the dressing before serving and enjoy.

Sweet Potato Fritters with Spicy Ketchup Sauce

This tasty sweet potato delicacy is a perfect snack for your kids during the day. You get the perfect energy kick from this snack. What's more? It is simple to prepare and will cater to your snacking needs throughout the day. For a better experience, mix the hot chili and ketchup.

Serving Size: 6

Cooking Time: 1 hour 30 minutes

Ingredients:

Fritters:

- 3 medium-sized sweet potatoes
- 2 tbsp melted butter
- 1/2 tsp salt
- 3/4 cup grated parmesan cheese
- 1/2 tsp pepper
- 2 cups sweet potato chips crumbs

Sauce:

- 1/2 cup ketchup
- 2 tbsp of hot chili sauce

Instructions:

Preheat your oven to 400°F. Prick the sweet potatoes to make some holes and bake for 60 minutes till tender. Set aside for 10 minutes to cool.

Peel the prebaked sweet potatoes by hand. In a medium-sized bowl, put in the sweet potatoes and mash properly with butter. Mix in the salt, parmesan cheese, and pepper to taste.

Have a baking sheet, drizzle the olive oil, and set aside. Take a shallow bowl and add the sweet potato (crumbs). Make a cylinder roll out of 1 tbsp of the sweet potato mixture. Add the chip into the roll and cover it on the baking sheet. Repeat the process till you finish the sweet potato mixture. Spray your fritters with the cooking spray, then sprinkle it with the parmesan cheese.

Bake the fritters for 15 minutes, flip over and proceed for another 15 minutes till crisp and golden. Remove it from the oven and serve with spicy ketchup.

Sweet Potato Pie

Nothing beats a sweet potato pie once winter starts setting in. Always enjoy your sweet potatoes through this baked pie. You and the present company will enjoy this enchanting fall treat. For a better experience, augment the pie with whipped cream or maple syrup.

Serving Size: 8

Cooking Time: 90 minutes

Ingredients:

- 1 tsp salt
- ⅔ tsp cinnamon
- 1 cup plain flour
- ⅓ cup butter
- 1½ cups brown sugar
- 1½ cups mashed sweet potato
- ¼ tsp nutmeg
- ½ cup maple syrup
- 3 eggs
- ½ cup pumpkin seeds
- ½ tsp ginger

Instructions:

Put the oven settings to preheat 350°F. Line the tart with baking paper.

Mix the pinch of salt and flour and sift properly. Add in the butter to make breadcrumb-like shapes. Add very little water slowly and shape the dough into an oblong-shaped ball.

Flatten the dough to about a ¼-inch thickness and put it in the tin.

Beat to mix the brown sugar, mashed sweet potato, cinnamon, nutmeg, and ginger. Add into the mixture the maple syrup and eggs and stir to get a well-balanced mix.

On top of the pie crust, pour out an even layer of filling and bake for 60 minutes. Insert a knife to check if ready. Bake for 30 minutes. Sprinkle atop the pie the pumpkin seeds.

Remove the pie and serve to enjoy.

Sweet Potato and Carrot Soup

The sweet potato and carrot soup is a delectable and nutritious soup that you and your family will enjoy.

Cooking Time: 30 Minutes

Serving Size: 4

Ingredients:

- 1 tbsp olive oil
- 3 tbsp minced garlic
- 1 diced yellow onion
- 2 tsp cumin
- 2 cups whole baby carrots
- 1 tbsp curry powder
- 4 cups chicken broth
- 2 cups cubed sweet potatoes

Instructions:

On a stove, put a saucepan with oil and heat at medium-high heat. Add the garlic and onion and sauté till the onions turn translucent.

Add the cumin, carrots, curry powder, sweet potatoes, and broth, and bring the mixture to a boil. Reduce the heat and cover to simmer (20 minutes).

Remove the resulting dish from the stove and puree.

Loaded Sweet Potatoes

A meal loaded with calories made by puffing the sweet potatoes with coleslaw. It won't cost your diet practices when you enjoy this delicacy once in a while.

Serving Size: 8

Cooking Time: 6 hours 15 minutes

Ingredients:

- 1 tsp cayenne pepper
- 1 tbsp brown sugar
- ½ tsp salt
- 1 tsp garlic powder
- 1/2 cup Dijon mustard, divided
- 4 roasted and shredded beef
- 1 cup beef broth
- 8 medium sweet potatoes
- 3 cups coleslaw mix
- 1/4 tsp garlic salt
- 1/2 tsp celery seed
- 1/2 cup mayonnaise
- 1/2 cup plain Greek yogurt
- 2 tbsp cider vinegar

Instructions:

Preheat your oven to 400°F. Meanwhile, put the pork in a slow cooker.

Into a small bowl, mix in cayenne, brown sugar, ¼ tsp of salt, garlic powder, 1/3 cup of mustard. Brush the resulting mixture over the meat.

Add the beef broth and cover to simmer for 6 hours till tender.

Back to your oven, scrub and poke the potatoes using a fork and bake for 45 minutes.

Into a large bowl, put in the coleslaw mixture.

Whisk the mustard, salt, garlic, celery, mayonnaise, yogurt, and vinegar into a separate small bowl. Pour this mixture over the coleslaw mixture and toss to mix.

Set aside the roast to cool and shred the meat with two forks.

Have the shredded meat back to the slow cooker. Meanwhile, make X-shapes onto each potato using a sharp knife and fluff the pulps using a fork.

Put the meat and the coleslaw mixtures on each potato using a slotted spoon.

Serve and enjoy.

Sweet Potato Milkshake

The sweet potato milkshake is a healthy and nutritious shake for those busy and exhausting days. You will need the burst of energy but more importantly, appreciate its exquisite taste. It takes a while to prepare, so always prepare more and refrigerate for future use.

Serving Size: 1

Cooking Time: 10 minutes

Ingredients:

- 1 small sweet potato
- 1 ½ cups skim milk
- 1 tsp pumpkin pie
- 1 scoop vanilla whey protein powder

Instructions:

For the best result, cook the sweet potato night before. Wash it well, pierce it using fork and microwave for 8-10 minutes and flip it over once.

Keep in the refrigerator to keep it cool.

If you want to make the shake, remove the skin of the sweet potato.

Blend together all the ingredients until the mixture is soft. Enjoy!

Sweet Potatoes Filled with Cranberry and Walnuts

Prepare these incredible sweet potatoes on your weekends and enjoy the flavors of walnuts and cranberry mixed with sweet potatoes.

Serving Size: 8

Cooking Time: 1 hour 25 minutes

Ingredients:

- 4 sweet potatoes
- 1 tbsp butter
- 1/4 cup chopped onion
- 1/4 tsp salt (divided)
- 1/4 cup cranberry juice
- 1/3 cup maple syrup
- 1 cup cranberries
- 1 tsp Dijon mustard
- 1/2 cup chopped and toasted walnuts
- 1/4 tsp pepper
- 2 tbsp minced chives

Instructions:

Put the oven settings to preheat at 400°F, make some holes on the sweet potatoes and bake them until tender, for 1 hour.

Have a small saucepan with butter over medium flame, then cook the onions until soft.

Add the syrup, cranberry juice, 1/8 teaspoon salt, and cranberries.

Allow to boil, then simmer while covered for 15 minutes as you stir occasionally.

Add the walnuts and mustard and stir for a few minutes, then allow to cool.

Cut the potatoes into halves lengthwise, then sprinkle pepper and the remaining salt.

Serve topped with chopped chives and the cranberry mixture.

Peanut Sweet Potato Stew

The African Peanut Sweet Potato stew is an exquisite and rich dish that will get you addicted in no time. You are going to love the sweet and pleasant taste of the soup.

Serving Size: 8

Cooking Time: 6 hours 20 minutes

Ingredients:

- ¼ tsp smoked paprika
- ½ tsp ground cinnamon
- 1 tsp salt
- 2 tsp ground cumin
- ½ cup chunky peanut butter
- 1 cup chopped cilantro
- 3½ cups diced tomatoes
- 1 cup water
- 2 cups rinsed and drained Garbanzo beans
- 6 cubed sweet potatoes
- 8 cups chopped kale
- Extra cilantro leaves as desired for serving
- Chopped peanuts as needed for serving

Instructions:

Place the first seven ingredients processed in a food processor, then pour into a five-quart slow cooker.

Add in sweet potatoes, beans, and water, and stir.

Cook on low while covered for 6 hours.

Stir in the kale 30 in the last 30 minutes.

Serve topped with chopped pecans and additional cilantro.

Baked Twice Sweet Potatoes

A definite try for anyone who loves exploring different kinds of recipes. These twice-baked sweet potatoes will surprise you and become a favorite in no time.

Serving Size: 4

Cooking Time: 60 minutes

Ingredients:

- 4 sweet potatoes
- 3 tbsp brown sugar
- 4 oz. cream cheese
- ½ tsp cinnamon
- 1 tsp salt
- ½ tsp black pepper

Instructions:

Preheat the oven to 375°

Have the sweet potatoes on a sheet pan and bake for 45 minutes, or until tender.

Halve the potatoes open and scoop out the innards.

Use a hand mixer to combine the sweet potato innards with the brown sugar, cream cheese, cinnamon, salt, and black pepper.

Have the mixture back into the sweet potato skins.

Return the filled potatoes back to the oven and bake for an additional 15 minutes.

Sweet Potato Hash

Want a simple yet nutritious brunch for you and present company? The Sweet Potato Hash brunch is by far a superior option. It is rich in vegetables and has a way of lifting your spirits during your midmornings.

Serving Size: 4

Cooking Time: 40 minutes

Ingredients:

- 2 large sweet potatoes
- 6 tbsp olive oil
- ½ chopped red onion
- Black pepper to taste
- 1 chopped red pepper
- 2 minced garlic cloves
- Salt as needed
- 2 tsp smoked paprika
- 2 tbsp chopped parsley

Instructions:

Peel and cube the sweet potato, add to a saucepan of boiling water and simmer until it is tender. Drain the water and place the cubes on paper towels to dry out.

Begin heating 2 tbsp of olive oil in a pan. Chop the onion, red pepper, and garlic, add to the pan and sauté for 4 minutes.

Drizzle the veggies with salt and pepper, and then put them on a plate.

Re-coat the pan with the olive oil (remaining) and add the sweet potatoes, stirring until they're tender and browned on the outside. After 5 minutes or so, increase the heat to high for a few minutes to allow the potatoes to crisp on the outside.

Sprinkle the paprika onto the potatoes and add the vegetables back in. Allow everything to cook together for a further minute or two, and then sprinkle with the fresh parsley before serving.

Sweet Potato Burgers

This dish is the perfect burger option for vegetarians. It is nutritious and will leave you wanting more. What's more? It is a simple and quick snack fix for you and your present company.

Serving Size: 5

Cooking Time: 20 minutes

Ingredients:

- 15 oz. can cannellini beans
- 2 cups cooked and mashed sweet potatoes
- 1 tsp lemon pepper
- 1 tsp cayenne pepper
- ¼ cup flour
- 5 halved hamburger buns

Instructions:

In a large bowl, mash the beans, potato, lemon pepper, cayenne pepper, and flour together. Mix well.

Form the mashed ingredients into patties.

Coat a skillet with nonstick cooking spray.

Cook the patties over medium-high heat, flipping midway through to ensure even cooking.

Place on hamburger buns and serve.

Sweet Potato Salad with Honey-Lime Juices

The power-packed and delicious salad is a go-to salad option for everyone who loves sweet potatoes. It is simple and quick to fix for your enjoyment.

Serving Size: 2

Cooking Time: 15 minutes

Ingredients:

- 2 cups diced sweet potatoes
- 1 tbsp salt
- 150 g diced bacon
- 2 cups herbed croutons
- Snipped parsley
- 1 tbsp of olive oil

Dressing:

- 2 tbsp virgin olive oil
- Salt to taste
- 2 tbsp honey
- Juice of two limes
- Black Pepper to taste

Instructions:

Preheat oven to 375°F.

Sprinkle sweet potatoes with salt and olive oil. Put it in a baking pan and bake in the oven for 12-15 minutes.

Have a frying pan on fire and cook the bacon until it is lightly crisp while waiting for the sweet potatoes to cook.

When the bacon is already cooked, prepare the dressing together with the croutons. Put together all the ingredients.

Mix bacon, croutons, and some parsley when sweet potatoes are already cooked. Sprinkle with honey dressing. Serve.

Sweet Potato Au Gratin

The simple-to-make sweet potato casserole is nutritious and delicious. You can never go wrong with this casserole for your family. A definite must-have in your recipe repertoire.

Serving Size: 6

Cooking Time: 50 minutes

Ingredients:

- 1 cup milk
- ½ tsp cinnamon
- 1 tsp salt
- 2 cups heavy cream
- 6 sliced sweet potatoes
- 2 tbsp melted butter
- 1/3 cup breadcrumbs
- 1/3 cup shredded cheddar cheese

Instructions:

Put the oven settings to preheat at 350°

Have a saucepan, stir the milk, heavy cream, cinnamon, and salt over medium heat.

Allow to simmer, then add the sweet potatoes, stirring occasionally.

Transfer to an oiled casserole dish.

Have a separate bowl, stir together the butter, breadcrumbs, and cheese.

Sprinkle the mixture over the potatoes, then bake in the ready oven for 40 minutes.

Orange Beef with Sweet Potatoes

The taste explosion from a mix of spice and sweet is always unrivaled, and this makes this dish an astonishing option. Glaze the delicacy with orange for a more stunning taste.

Serving Size: 6

Cooking Time: 1 hour 15 minutes

Ingredients:

- 2 sliced apples
- 2 sliced sweet potatoes
- 1 sliced orange
- 1/2 tsp pepper
- 1 tsp salt
- 1 tsp crushed ginger
- 1 tsp ground cinnamon
- 2 tsp cornstarch
- 2 tbsp brown sugar
- 2 beef tenderloins
- 1 cup orange juice

Instructions:

Put the oven settings to preheat at 350°

Have the sliced apples, potatoes, and oranges on a baking tray filled with foil and coated with cooking spray.

Drizzle some salt and pepper, then roast them for 10 minutes.

Have a microwave-safe bowl and mix brown sugar, ginger, cornstarch, cinnamon, and orange juice, then microwave for 2 minutes on high.

Stir the mixture until soft.

Place the beef over sweet potato mixture, then pour the orange mixture over and roast for 55 minutes.

Put it aside for 8 minutes to rest before serving.

Grilled Three-Potato Salad

This dish is a delicious potato salad that brings a luscious tinge to the conventional potato salad. This dish is a must-try for you and your family.

Serving Size: 6

Cooking Time: 35 minutes

Ingredients:

- 1 sweet potato
- 1¾ red potatoes
- 1¾ cups Yukon gold potatoes
- 1/ cups sliced green onions
- 1/4 tsp pepper
- 1/2 tsp celery seed
- 1 tsp salt
- 1 tbsp Dijon mustard
- 3 tbsp white wine vinegar
- 1/4 cup canola oil

Instructions:

Place the sweet potato, Yukon gold potatoes, and red potatoes in a Dutch oven and simmer until tender for 20 minutes while covered.

Drain the liquid, leave to cool, then chop into chunks.

Add the potato mixture to a basket or a grill wok and grill for 12 minutes until browned evenly.

Have the mixture into a large salad bowl and add the onions.

Have another bowl and whisk together oil, vinegar, mustard, salt, celery seed, and pepper, then pour over the potato mixture.

Toss to coat evenly and serve.

Sweet Potato with Curry Powder

The sweet potato with curry dish comes as a healthy, nutritious, creamy, and vegan curry option. This simple-to-make dish only takes 35 minutes for you and present company to enjoy. You can serve with rice as a side dish.

Serving Size: 6

Cooking Time: 25 minutes

Ingredients:

- 2 tsp curry powder
- 3 tbsp olive oil
- 2 grated onions
- 1 grated apple
- 20 g chopped coriander
- 3 crushed garlic cloves
- 1 grated ginger root
- 800 g sweet potatoes
- 100 g red lentils
- 2 liters vegetable stock
- 300 ml milk
- 1 lime juice

Instructions:

In a large saucepan, put the curry powder and toast over medium heat for 2 minutes. Put olive oil and stir in the pan. Gently cook the onions, apple, coriander stalks, garlic, and ginger.

Peel the sweet potato and grate it. Put together the lentils, stock, milk, and seasoning in the pan, let it simmer for 20 minutes, and cover. Blend until soft with a stick blender. Mix the lime juice and serve. Put some roughly-cut coriander leaves on top.

Sweet Potato Casserole

The sweet potato casserole is a holiday stalwart for almost everyone I know. You can easily modify this dish to accommodate distinct tastes as you desire.

Serving Size: 16

Cooking Time: 55 minutes

Ingredients:

- 2 cubed sweet potatoes
- 1/3 cup white sugar
- 2 eggs
- 1/4 tsp salt
- 6 tbsp melted butter, divided
- 1/3 cup milk
- 1/4 tsp vanilla
- 1/3 cup brown sugar
- 1/4 cup flour
- 1/3 cup crushed walnuts

Instructions:

Preheat the oven to 350°F.

Boil the sweet potatoes covered with water in a saucepan over high heat until the pieces are tender. Drain and puree.

Combine the pureed sweet potatoes, white sugar, eggs, salt, butter, milk, and vanilla in a bowl.

Mix until even, then pour into a greased casserole dish.

Stir together the brown sugar, flour, 3 tbsp reserved butter, and walnuts in a separate bowl.

Sprinkle over the casserole dish.

Bake in the ready oven for 40 minutes.

Baked Sweet Potato with Nutmeg

This delicious dish comes topped with crushed nutmeg to give it that soft kick. Kickstart your day with this delicacy.

Serving Size: 8

Cooking Time: 35 minutes

Ingredients:

- 1/2 cup orange juice
- 3 tbsp molasses
- 1/4 tsp nutmeg
- 5 sweet potatoes, sliced
- 1/4 tsp salt
- 1/4 tsp black pepper
- 2 tbsp olive oil
- 2 tbsp butter

Instructions:

Preheat oven to 400°F.

Mix orange juice, molasses, and nutmeg in a small bowl. Set aside mixture.

Combine sweet potatoes, salt, pepper, and olive oil in a large bowl. Cover the potatoes.

On the baking sheet, put sweet potatoes in a single layer.

Roast the sweet potatoes for 15 minutes.

Flip sweet potatoes over, then brush with half of the orange juice mixture.

Preheat the sweet potatoes in the oven to continue roasting for 7-10 minutes until they get tender.

Put together the remaining orange juice mixture and butter in a small saucepan. Beat over medium to high heat for 10 minutes until the mixture thickens.

In a large serving dish, place the sweet potatoes and mix with butter and orange juice glaze.

Chili Bake Sweet Potato

Are you a vegetarian? then try and enjoy the flavor and aroma is this chili bake made with sweet potatoes.

Serving Size: 7

Cooking Time: 50 minutes

Ingredients:

- 1 chopped sweet red pepper
- 2 cups cubed sweet potato
- 1 tbsp olive oil
- 1 minced garlic clove
- ½ tsp pepper
- 1 chopped jalapeno pepper
- 1 tsp salt
- 3 tbsp chili powder
- 4 ½ tsp brown sugar
- 2 cups black beans
- 2 cups vegetable broth
- 3 ½ cups diced tomatoes
- 1 oz. shredded cheddar cheese
- ½ cup sour cream
- ¾ cup muffin mix

Instructions:

Have a Dutch oven in place with oil to heat, then cook sweet potatoes and red pepper until tender.

Stir in the garlic for a minute.

Add tomatoes, broth, beans, jalapeno pepper, brown sugar, chili powder, salt, sour cream, and pepper to boil, then simmer for 20 minutes.

Put the oven settings to preheat at 400°

Make the muffin mix as per the package guidelines, then stir in the cheddar cheese.

Add the muffin mix mixture into the chili.

Bake in the ready oven while covered for 20 minutes and serve with your preferred toppings.

Sweet Potato Scones

Sweet potatoes in your scone avert the disappointment that stems at times when biting a conventional scone. The scones have a delectable taste, come nutritious and one you will enjoy with present company. Sprinkle some brown sugar cream for extra taste.

Serving Size: 12

Cooking Time: 90 minutes

Ingredients:

- 13 oz. sweet potato
- 1 ½ oz. maple syrup
- 1 egg
- 2 oz. ground almonds
- 1 oz. caster sugar
- ½ tsp baking powder
- ½ cup sultanas
- ¼ tsp nutmeg
- ½ tsp cinnamon
- 2 ½ oz. butter
- 7 oz. plain flour
- 1 tsp salt

Instructions:

Put the oven settings to preheat at 390°F and line a baking tray with parchment paper.

Enclose the sweet potatoes in foil and bake in the oven until tender, roughly an hour.

Halve the potatoes lengthways, and once cool enough to handle, scoop out all of the softened flesh.

Blend the sweet potato flesh, maple syrup, and egg until smooth.

Separately, mix the ground almonds, sugar, plain flour, salt, baking powder, sultanas, nutmeg and cinnamon.

Rub in the butter to create a texture like that of breadcrumbs.

Little by little, add the sweet potatoes mixture, stirring well to create a moist but not sticky dough. Beware that you may not need to use all of the sweet potato mix to achieve this.

Flour a surface lightly and begin to roll the dough out to a 1-inch thickness.

Cut out your scones.

Place the scones in the baking tray and bake for 12-15 minutes, until golden brown.

Curried Sweet Potato Wedges

Curried sweet potato wedges are an excellent way of impressing your guests. It is a quick fix that will give you plenty of time to enjoy it with your guests or family. The smoked paprika and curry give it a tasty and unforgettable edge.

Serving Size: 4

Cooking Time: 25 minutes

Ingredients:

- 2 sweet potatoes, cut into wedges
- 1/8 tsp black pepper
- ½ tsp smoked paprika
- 1 tsp curry powder
- ½ tsp salt
- 2 tbsp olive oil
- 1 tbsp minced cilantro
- Mango chutney as needed

Instructions:

Put the oven settings to preheat at 425°F and place the sweet potatoes into a large-sized bowl.

Combine the seasonings and oil, then drizzle on the sweet potatoes, tossing to coat evenly, and put them on a baking pan.

Roast until tender, for 20 minutes, turning frequently.

Serve sprinkled with cilantro and mango chutney.

Sweet Potato Soufflé

The sweet potato soufflé has a way around it to fool your guests on the potential labor directed at making them. What's more? It is tasty and nutritionally rich.

Serving Size: 8

Cooking Time: 1 hour 55 minutes

Ingredients:

- 4 cups cubed sweet potatoes
- 6 tbsp softened butter
- ¾ cup evaporated milk
- 2 eggs
- ½ cup brown sugar
- 1 tbsp baking powder
- 2 cups marshmallow fluff

Instructions:

Preheat the oven to 350°

In a saucepan, boil the sweet potatoes over medium-high heat until the pieces are tender. Remove from heat, drain, and puree.

Stir in the butter, evaporated milk, eggs, brown sugar, and baking powder.

Grease six ramekins and set them on a sheet pan.

Spoon in the potato mixture until the ramekins are 1 inch from being full. Bake for 30 minutes.

Remove from the oven and spoon the marshmallow fluff into each ramekin.

Return to the oven, continuing to bake until the marshmallow fluff browns.

Slow Cooker Sweet Potato Soup

It is a tasty and confounding soup in that you can substitute the toppings in line with your taste and flavors.

Serving Size: 8

Cooking Time: 5 hours 15 minutes

Ingredients:

- 6 cups chicken broth
- 1/8 tsp ground chipotle pepper
- ¼ tsp dried thyme
- ½ tsp black pepper
- 1 tsp dried celery flakes
- ½ tsp salt
- 1 minced onion
- 1 tbsp Worcestershire sauce
- 2 tbsp Butter
- 8 cups cubed sweet potatoes
- Pepitas as needed
- ½ cup sour cream

Instructions:

Add all the ingredients, leaving sour cream and pepitas to a 5-quart slow cooker, then cook while covered for 6 hours on low.

Pulse the soup in a blender after cooling slightly in batches, then pour it back in the slow cooker to heat through.

Serve topped with pepitas and sour cream.

Sweet Potato and Egg Skillet

I have never experienced a more wholesome and nourishing meal than the sweet potato and egg skillet. It is equally mouthwatering and can serve you and the present company.

Serving Size: 4

Cooking Time: 25 minutes

Ingredients:

- 2 tbsp butter
- 1/8 tsp dried thyme
- 1/2 tsp salt, divided
- 1 minced garlic clove
- 4 cups shredded sweet potatoes
- 2 cups baby spinach
- 4 eggs
- 1/8 tsp black pepper

Instructions:

Have a heavy skillet with butter over low heat to melt, then cook sweet potatoes, garlic, ¼ teaspoon salt, and thyme while covered for 5 minutes as you stir.

Stir in the spinach for 3 minutes.

Make four holes in the potato mixture in a skillet and break one egg in each hole.

Drizzle the remaining salt, pepper on the eggs, and cook while covered for 7 minutes over medium-low heat.

Sweet Potato Chips

Are you addicted to unhealthy potato fries? Try these nutritious and healthy sweet potato chips. You will be hooked for life.

Serving Size: 4

Cooking Time: 30 minutes

Ingredients:

- 2 sliced sweet potatoes
- 1 tbsp olive oil
- 1 tsp sea salt

Instructions:

Preheat the oven to 400°

In a bowl, toss oil, sweet potatoes, and salt together to ensure even coating.

Have a sheet pan with aluminum foil, then place the sweet potato slices on the pan.

Bake for 35 minutes, flipping halfway through, or until the chips are crispy.

Curried Chicken and Sweet Potatoes

The curried chicken and sweet potato dish combine a simplicity to prepare and a rich nutritional profile.

Serving Size: 3

Cooking Time: 1 hour 15 minutes

Ingredients:

- 1 lb. stripped boneless chicken breast
- 3 tbsp curry powder
- 1 tsp salt
- 2 tbsp olive oil
- 1 diced yellow onion
- 1 tbsp minced garlic
- 1 tsp red pepper flakes
- 1 cup chicken broth
- ½ cup diced carrot
- 1 cup milk
- 2 cups cubed and peeled sweet potatoes

Instructions:

Coat the chicken with curry powder and salt.

Heat the oil in a large skillet over a medium-high temperature.

Fry the garlic and onion until the onion becomes translucent.

Add the red pepper flakes and chicken, cooking until the chicken is browned.

Pour in the broth and add the carrots, cooking for an additional 10 minutes.

Stir in the milk and sweet potatoes.

Simmer until the chicken is cooked well and the vegetables are tender.

Sweet Potato Mashed with Maple Syrup

This delicious and nutritious delicacy is perfect for starting your busy day. It also has a pleasant taste that you and your kids will enjoy.

Serving Size: 8

Cooking Time: 55 minutes

Ingredients:

- 4 lb. sweet potatoes
- 2 tbsp butter
- 2 tbsp pure maple syrup
- 1 tbsp chili powder
- 2 tbsp toasted and ground cumin seeds
- 1 tsp salt
- 1/2 tsp black pepper

Instructions:

Preheat oven to 350°F.

Pierce sweet potato using a fork. Put on the oven and bake for 45 minutes to 1 hour until soft.

Place it into a cutting board and let it cool for 10 minutes.

Remove sweet potatoes skins and slice into 1 inch and put to a bowl.

Smash the potatoes until they soften.

Put together the butter, pepper, chili powder, ground cumin, salt, and maple syrup.

Sweet Potato Burritos

The sweet potato burrito is a delicious and fulfilling vegetable filling that you'll get hooked on once you try it out. It is nutritious and the perfect snack for you.

Serving Size: 4

Cooking Time: 55 minutes

Ingredients:

- 1 tbsp canola oil
- 3 cups mashed sweet potatoes
- 1 diced yellow onion
- 2 tbsp minced garlic
- 3 cups black beans
- 1 cup water
- 2 tbsp chili powder
- 1 tsp cumin
- 1 tsp cayenne pepper
- 2 tbsp soy sauce
- 10 flour tortillas
- 1 cup cheddar cheese

Instructions:

Put the oven settings to preheat at 350°

Have a skillet with oil over medium-high heat.

Fry the garlic and onion until the onion is translucent.

Add the black beans and water, stirring until the beans are heated through.

Combine the soy sauce, chili powder, cayenne pepper, and cumin.

Remove from heat and puree.

Spread the bean combination and the mashed sweet potatoes over the tortillas.

Place the burritos seam side down in a greased casserole dish.

Sprinkle the cheese over the burritos.

Bake in the ready oven for 14 minutes or until cheese is melted.

Sausage-Sweet Potato Hash and Eggs

This is an easy-to-make delicacy with a wonderful rousing taste and a confounding texture. You will surely enjoy this one.

Serving Size: 4

Cooking Time: 25 minutes

Ingredients:

- 2 cubed sweet potatoes
- 4 and 1/8 cups Italian turkey sausage links (without casings)
- 1/4 tsp salt
- 1/4 cup chopped pecans
- 1/4 cup dried cranberries
- 2 granny smith apples
- 4 sliced green onions
- 4 large eggs

Instructions:

Have a large skillet coated with cooking spray on medium fire, then cook the sausages and sweet potatoes for 10 minutes as you crumble the sausage.

Mix in the apple, cranberries, pecans, and salt to cook for 6 minutes.

Have the mixture from the pan and keep it warm, sprinkled with green onions.

On the same skillet, wipe it, coat with cooking spray, and adjust the heat to medium-high.

Break the eggs on the hot pan, then put the heat on low and cook until the whites settle, then turn and cook to your desired doneness and serve with the hash.

Cinnamon Spiced Sweet Potato Fries

This spicy-sweet potato is an ideal snack or brunch. It has a rich cinnamon flavor and is simple to prepare.

Serving Size: 4

Cooking Time: 30 minutes

Ingredients:

- 1 and 1/2 lbs. stripped sweet potatoes
- 2 tbsp olive oil
- 1 tsp. ground cinnamon
- Salt as needed
- Black pepper to taste
- 1/8 tsp ground cumin

Instructions:

Preheat oven to 400°F. Place a heavy-duty sheet tray into the oven to heat.

In a large bowl, add sweet potatoes and drizzle with olive oil. Mix with cinnamon, salt, pepper, and cumin.

Spread out the sweet potatoes in the hot tray and bake until crisp for 25 to 30 minutes. Flip the fries once when roasting.

Roasted Sweet Potatoes with Pasta

These buttery and rich cream sauce-coated sweet potatoes are perfect for your family or visiting friends. Enjoy the outstanding flavor and nutritional profile.

Serving Size: 7

Cooking Time: 40 minutes

Ingredients:

- 1 sliced onion
- 3 cubed sweet potatoes
- 1/8 tsp pepper
- 1/2 tsp dried sage leaves
- 3/4 tsp salt
- 1 tbsp olive oil
- 3 minced garlic cloves
- 2 cups uncooked rigatoni
- 2 tbsp butter
- 1/2 cup chicken broth
- 1 cup heavy whipping cream
- 1/2 cup toasted and chopped walnuts
- Parmesan cheese as needed for serving

Instructions:

Place the sweet potatoes and onions in a baking pan.

Combine the garlic, oil, salt, sage, and Pepper, then toss on the vegetables to coat evenly.

Bake in a ready oven for 25 minutes, uncovered at 400°F, as you stir occasionally.

Follow the guidelines on the rigatoni package as you cook them.

Have a medium saucepan with butter on fire to melt, stir in cream and chicken broth to boil, then cook for 12 minutes.

Drain the rigatoni, then have them in a large bowl.

Mix in the vegetables, cream sauce, and walnuts until even, then serve topped with cheese.

Dairy-Free Sweet Potato Ice Cream

Ever crave a sweet potato pie, but it's too hot outside? Try this sweet potato ice cream. It offers the perfect simple and refreshing remedy for your craving in sweltering weather. It is also simple to prepare! For a better experience, add bourbon whiskey and pecans as a topping.

Serving Size: 6

Cooking Time: 60 minutes

Ingredients:

- 1 large sweet potato
- 1 cup cashews, pre-soaked overnight
- 1 cup almond milk
- ½ cup maple syrup
- ½ tsp cinnamon
- ½ tsp ginger
- ¼ tsp nutmeg
- 1 tsp salt
- Pecans as needed for topping
- Bourbon whiskey as needed for topping

Instructions:

Preheat the oven to 400°F and stab the potato a few times with a fork before wrapping in foil. Bake for 40-50 minutes until tender.

Drain the cashews and pulse them together with the almond milk, maple syrup, cinnamon, ginger, nutmeg and a pinch of salt.

Have the skin removed from the sweet potato, add it to the mix and blend until smooth.

Freeze overnight in a freezer-safe container before serving.

Serve topped with a shot of bourbon and pecans.

Sweet Potato Cheesecake

It is a creamy delicacy primarily used as dessert. You can impress your family and any present company with this sweet potato cheesecake.

Serving Size: 12

Cooking Time: 40 minutes

Ingredients:

- 16 oz. cream cheese
- 1 cup cooked and mashed sweet potatoes
- ½ cup sugar
- ½ tsp cinnamon
- ½ tsp vanilla
- 2 eggs
- 1 (9-inch) premade piecrust

Instructions:

Preheat the oven to 400°F and stab the potato a few times with a fork before wrapping it in foil. Bake for 40-50 minutes until tender.

Drain the cashews and pulse them with almond milk, maple syrup, cinnamon, ginger, nutmeg, and a pinch of salt.

Have the skin removed from the sweet potato, add it to the mix and blend until smooth.

Freeze overnight in a freezer-safe container before serving.

Serve topped with a shot of bourbon and pecans.

Sweet Potato Patties

Do you have leftover sweet potatoes and have no ideas on how to use them? The sweet potato patties offer an excellent way of making good use of such leftovers. The delicacy is nutritious, simple to make, and tasty.

Serving Size: 14

Cooking Time: 30 minutes

Ingredients:

- 4 tbsp olive oil
- 4 cups mashed sweet potatoes
- 1 cup diced yellow onion
- 1 egg
- ½ cup breadcrumbs
- 1 tbsp dried rosemary
- Salt as needed
- Black Pepper to taste

Instructions:

Heat a skillet with oil over medium heat.

In a bowl, mix the mashed sweet potatoes, onion, egg, breadcrumbs, and rosemary.

Spoon the mixture into the hot oil.

Flip to cook evenly on both sides.

Add some pepper and salt. Serve.

Sweet Potato and Kale Cannellini Soup

This astonishing and iconic mix of spices and sweet flavors will have you glued forever. The delicacy can serve you and any present company.

Serving Size: 12

Cooking Time: 1 hour 5 minutes

Ingredients:

- 1 chopped onion
- 3 minced garlic cloves
- 1¾ cups vegetable broth
- 1 cup shredded parmesan cheese
- 1/2 cup giardiniera
- ¼ tsp black pepper
- ½ tsp salt
- 1 tsp crushed red pepper flakes
- 1 tsp rubbed sage
- 2 tbsp olive oil
- 1 tsp honey
- 2 chopped apples
- 5 cubed sweet potatoes
- 3 cups chopped kale
- 2 cups rinsed and drained cannellini beans
- ½ cup heavy whipping cream

Instructions:

In a stockpot with oil over medium fire, cook the onions for 7 minutes, until soft.

Mix the garlic for a minute, then add broth, apples, honey, seasonings, and sweet potatoes.

Allow to boil, then simmer for 1 hour 30 minutes.

Pulse the soup in the immersion blender, then pour it back to the pan to heat.

Stir in the beans, kale, and giardiniera. Cook over medium heat for 15 minutes uncovered as you stir.

Mix in the cream and parmesan cheese, then serve with your preferred toppings.

Sweet Potato with Pecan Topping

The classic holiday delicacy is a popular choice for many holidaymakers. You can bring the holidaying mood into your house with this dish. What's more? It is simple to prepare and can serve you and the present company.

Serving Size: 15

Cooking Time: 1 hour

Ingredients:

- 3 cups cooked and mashed sweet potatoes
- 1 tsp vanilla extract
- 2 eggs
- 1/3 cup melted butter
- 1 cup white sugar

Topping:

- 1 cup chopped pecans
- 1/3 cup cold butter
- 1 cup shredded coconut
- 1 cup brown sugar
- 1/3 cup all-purpose flour

Instructions:

In a large pot, boil the sweet potatoes and cook for 40 minutes until done. Remove and peel the skin.

Mash using an electric mixer until fairly smooth. Combine the vanilla extract, eggs, butter, and sugar.

Add topping ingredients in a bowl and mix until even.

Drizzle the mixture of the topping ingredients on top of sweet potatoes and bake in the ready oven at 350°F for 30 minutes and serve.

Sweet Potato, Spinach, and Lentil Dahl

This traditional Indian is a treat you must try as a sweet potato lover. It has lentils and spinach to complete the sweet potato dish. It is the easy perfect winter warmer for those cold evenings.

Serving Size: 4

Cooking Time: 40 minutes

Ingredients:

- 1 red onion, diced
- 1 garlic clove, chopped
- 2 inches chopped ginger
- 1 chopped red chili
- 2 cups vegetable stock
- 1½ tsp turmeric
- 1½ tsp cumin
- 2 sweet potatoes, diced
- 2¾ oz. split red lentils
- 2¾ oz. spinach
- 1 bunch fresh basil leaves

Instructions:

In a large pan with oil, cook the red onion on low heat for a few minutes.

Add the chopped chili, ginger, and garlic to cook for 2 minutes.

Mix in the turmeric and cumin and cook down for another minute.

Add the diced sweet potatoes, stirring well, and turn the heat up to medium.

Add in the lentils and vegetable stock. Bring to a boil and then cover the pot, reduce the heat, leave it to simmer, and reduce it for 20 minutes. The lentils and potatoes should both be tender but still retain their shapes.

Then, add in the spinach. After a minute or so, serve with the torn basil leaves as a garnish once the spinach has wilted.

Sweet Potato Rolls

If you are craving a unique, simple, ad wholesome roll, sweet potato rolls will work a treat. These delicious and nutritious delicacies will not only serve you but any present company as well.

Serving Size: 15

Cooking Time: 2 hours 25 minutes

Ingredients:

- ¼ oz. dry active yeast
- ½ cup warm water
- 4 tbsp sugar, divided
- ½ cup pureed sweet potato
- 3 tbsp melted butter
- 1 tsp salt
- 2 eggs
- 4 cups flour

Instructions:

Stir the yeast, water, and 1 tbsp sugar in a bowl.

Let stand for several minutes, then add the 3 tbsp of reserved sugar, sweet potato, butter, salt, eggs, and flour. Mix well.

Leave the dough to rise while covered for 1 hour.

Preheat the oven to 375°

Roll the dough into balls and place it on an oiled sheet pan.

Bake for 15 minutes.

Sweet Potato, Avocado, and Feta Muffins

The simple matter of lacking a sweet tooth does not imply you are missing these moist, crumbly, and savory baking. The avocado provides it the incredible texture, whereas the toppings give it its savory taste.

Serving Size: 9

Cooking Time: 45 minutes

Ingredients:

- 1 ¾ oz. feta cheese
- 1 sweet potato
- 1 large avocado
- 3¼ oz. skimmed milk
- 3½ oz. ground almonds
- 3½ oz. fine polenta
- 3 eggs
- 1½ tsp baking powder
- 1 tsp bicarbonate of soda
- ¾ cup maple syrup
- 1 tsp salt
- ¼ tsp. sweet paprika
- 2 tbsp mixed seeds

Instructions:

Peel and dice the sweet potato. Please in a heatproof bowl and cover with the cling wrap. Microwave on high for about 8-10 minutes.

Put the oven settings to preheat at 350°F and grease a muffin tin or line with muffin cases.

Peel and pit your avocado, add skimmed milk, and roughly mash with a fork.

Set ¼ of your cooked sweet potato aside and chop it even smaller. Add the rest to a bowl, along with the mashed avocado, ground almonds, polenta, eggs, baking powder, bicarbonate of soda, maple syrup, and a pinch of salt. Blend this mixture until smooth.

Have the mixture between the muffin cases evenly, and then top each with a little sweet potato, some crumbled feta, a dusting of paprika, and a sprinkling of mixed seeds.

Bake in the ready oven for 20-25 minutes, until browned on top.

Sweet Potato and Bean Quesadillas

The sweet potato and bean quesadilla are a fun, quick, simple, and delicious recipe with exceptional aroma and flavor.

Serving Size: 4

Cooking Time: 30 minutes

Ingredients:

- 2 medium sweet potatoes
- 4 whole-wheat tortillas
- 1/2 cup shredded pepper Jack cheese
- 3/4 cup drained and rinsed black beans
- 3/4 cup salsa

Instructions:

Make some holes on the sweet potatoes and microwave them on high for 9 minutes, turning once.

When cool enough, halve the sweet potatoes lengthwise.

Peel the pulp out of the potatoes and spread it onto half of all the tortillas.

Add on the cheese and beans, then fold half of the tortillas.

Have a skillet over medium heat and cook the filled quesadillas for 3 minutes on each side, then serve with salsa.

Sweet Potato Veggie Samosas

Do you love samosas? You will love these even more. Sweet potato samosas are delicious ad come packed with vegetables, fiber, etc., to cater to your family's nutritional needs.

Serving Size: 6

Cooking Time: 75 minutes

Ingredients:

- 2 large diced sweet potatoes
- 2 red onions
- 2 garlic cloves
- 2 inches fresh ginger
- 1 red chili
- Sunflower oil as needed
- 2 tbsp curry paste
- 2 tsp nigella seeds
- 7 oz. spinach
- 1 small bunch of fresh coriander
- 6 sheets pre-made filo pastry

Instructions:

Put the oven settings to preheat at 390°F and line a baking tray with parchment paper.

Add the diced sweet potatoes to a heatproof bowl.

Microwave for 8-10 minutes while covered until the potato is soft and tender.

Dice the onion, garlic, ginger, and chili.

Begin heating a little oil in a pan and add the onion. After 2-3 minutes, add the ginger and chili, and then the garlic a minute later. Stir well.

Add the curry paste and 1 tsp of nigella seeds to the pan.

Then, add the spinach along with 2-3 tbsp of water. Once the spinach is wilted, add in the sweet potato and mix everything.

Mash everything together roughly but leave some chunks of sweet potato for texture. Add some roughly chopped fresh coriander to the mix.

Take two filo sheets and lightly brush both sides of each with oil. Add a light sprinkling of nigella seeds to the side of one sheet and then place the second sheet on top. Cut down the middle lengthways to create 2 long strips.

Take 1/6 of the sweet potato mix and place in the top right-hand corner of the strip, leaving a little room around the edges. Arrange in a roughly triangular shape. Fold the pastry at an angle and continue doing so all the way down the strip so that you end up with the filling encased in a triangle of pastry.

Brush a little more oil on top of each samosa and sprinkle with any remaining nigella seeds. Bake for 25-30 minutes.

Sweet Potato Pancakes

The delicacy marks the changing seasons on the breakfast table. The sweet potato is nutritious and perfect for you and your kids before kick-starting your day.

Serving Size: 4

Cooking Time: 40 minutes

Ingredients:

- 1 cup sweet potato pie filling
- 2 eggs
- 2 cups milk
- ½ tsp vanilla
- 3 cups baking mix

Instructions:

Whisk together pie filling, eggs, milk, vanilla, and baking mix in a large bowl.

Coat a skillet with nonstick cooking spray, then pour in the pancake mix.

As you see the bubbles on the surface, flip to cook on the other side.

Remove from heat when cooked through.

Sweet Potato Hummus

Acquaint yourself with hummus, the middle-eastern taste. You can always do this through the sweet potato hummus delicacy. Humus represents a dip of versatile chickpea. Enjoy this dish with your family.

Serving Size: 4

Cooking Time: 25 minutes

Ingredients:

- 16 oz. sweet potatoes
- 1 crushed garlic clove
- 1 juiced lemon
- 19 oz. canned chickpeas, drained
- 2 tbsp olive oil
- 2 tsp cumin
- ¼ cup tahini paste
- 1 tsp salt
- Black pepper to taste

Instructions:

Set a large saucepan of water to simmer.

Peel and dice the sweet potatoes. Then, add them to the water and simmer for 8-12 minutes until a fork can easily be inserted.

Have the potatoes in a blender and add the drained chickpeas, olive oil, cumin, crushed garlic, lemon juice, and tahini paste.

Blend in pepper and salt, then serve.

Toast yourself some whole-wheat pita and get yourself a platter of chopped veggies, such as red pepper, cucumber, and carrots, and get dipping!

Sweet Potato Lentil Stew

The sweet potato lentil stew is spicy and tasty for you and your family to enjoy. You cannot compare it to other similar dishes.

Serving Size: 6

Cooking Time: 6 hours

Ingredients:

- 5 ¼ cups vegetable broth
- ¼ tsp cayenne pepper
- ¼ tsp ground ginger
- ½ tsp ground cumin
- 4 minced garlic cloves
- 1 chopped onion
- 1 chopped carrot
- 1½ cups dried lentils
- 2¼ cups chopped sweet potatoes
- ¼ cup minced cilantro

Instructions:

Take a 3-quart cooker (slow) and cook together the first nine ingredients without covering.

Cook on low flame for 6 hours until the lentils and vegetables become tender.

Mix into it the cilantro and serve.

Sweet Potato Smoothie

For all smoothie lovers, you cannot miss this healthy and exquisite sweet potato smoothie. You will get hooked for life.

Serving Size: 1

Preparation Time: 10 minutes

Ingredients:

- 2 cups cooked and mashed sweet potatoes
- 2 cups soymilk
- 1 cup ice
- 1 tsp vanilla
- 1 banana
- ½ tsp ginger powder

Instructions:

Combine the mashed sweet potatoes, soymilk, ice, vanilla, banana, and ginger in a food processor.

Pulse until the ingredients are completely mixed. Serve and enjoy.

Spiced Sweet Potato Bread

Imagine the sweet and homely aroma of freshly baked bread. What of a tinge of extra spice atop the fresh aroma? This spiced sweet potato bread provides you with that. You can enjoy it with your whole family. A little cold, fresh butter spread on this served with a c of fresh coffee is perfection.

Serving Size: 8

Cooking Time: 80 minutes

Ingredients:

- 2 sliced sweet potatoes, large
- ½ cup coconut flour
- 1 tsp baking powder
- 1 tsp baking soda
- 1 tbsp cinnamon
- 1 tsp nutmeg
- ½ tsp mace
- ¼ tsp salt
- ½ cup butter
- 6 tbsp coconut oil
- 4 eggs
- 1 tsp almond extract

Instructions:

Preheat the oven at 350°F and line a loaf tin with parchment paper.

Add the potato slices to a saucepan and cover with an inch of water to boil and cook for 5 minutes, until tender.

Remove all the liquid and mash them until soft.

Mix the coconut flour, baking powder, baking soda, cinnamon, nutmeg, mace, and a pinch of salt.

Have a microwave-safe bowl, melt the butter and coconut oil.

Combine the butter mix, eggs, mashed sweet potatoes, and almond extract, and mix well.

Mix in the flour mixture and then evenly pour the mix into the loaf tin.

Bake for 50-60 minutes until a toothpick can be inserted and come out clean.

Serve and enjoy!

Sweet Potato Crescents

The sweet potato crescents come in handy as snacks in functions. Prepare these light snacks and entertain your guests to the fullest.

Serving Size: 6

Cooking Time: 45 minutes

Ingredients:

- 1 cup warm water
- 1 tbsp active dry yeast
- 1½ tsp salt
- 5½ cups all-purpose flour
- 1 large egg
- 1/2 cup shortening
- ½ cup sugar
- 2 cups cooked and mashed sweet potatoes
- ¼ cup melted butter

Instructions:

In a large bowl, dissolve the yeast into the water and rest for 5 minutes.

Beat salt, shortening, 3 cups of flour, egg, sugar, and sweet potatoes.

Add more flour to form a stiff dough.

Knead the dough on a floured surface for 6 to 7 minutes until smooth and elastic, then have the dough in a greased bowl.

Allow it to sit for 1 hour to rise and double in volume.

Divide the dough into 12 wedges, brush them with butter, roll from wide end up, put them on a greased baking dish, cover, and leave them to rise and double in volume.

Bake in the ready oven at 375°F for 15 minutes.

Serve after cooling.

Shredded Sweet Potatoes with Beef

The Chipotle Shredded Sweet Potato with Beef possesses a pleasant smoky flavor that blends incredibly with the creamy and cheesy side dish. You will enjoy this dish with family or present company.

Serving Size: 10

Cooking Time: 4 hours 30 minutes

Ingredients:

- 4 shredded sweet potatoes
- 2 cups cooked and chopped beef
- 1/2 tsp paprika
- ½ tsp kosher salt
- 1 tsp ground pepper
- 2 tbsp olive oil
- 2 chopped shallots
- 1 chopped sweet onion
- ¼ minced parsley

Topping Ingredients:

- ¼ tsp ground chipotle pepper
- 2 tsp maple syrup
- 2 cups shredded Munster cheese
- 1¼ cup softened cream cheese
- 2 cups shredded Monterey Jack cheese
- 1 cup sour cream
- 2 tsp chipotle pepper

Instructions:

In a large skillet with oil over medium heat, cook the onions and shallots as you stir for 6 minutes until soft.

Add the onion mixture to a large-sized bowl and stir in the salt, pepper, and parsley.

Mix in the sweet potatoes and chopped meat until even.

Add the meat mixture to a greased slow cooker, then sprinkle with paprika and cook while covered for 6 hours.

In a mixing bowl, combine the topping ingredients and serve them with sweet potatoes.

Tasty Sweet Potato Skins

Stuffing your potato skin with bacon and cheese proves far superior to any other alternative of stuffing the potato skins. Enjoy this delicacy with friends and family.

Serving Size: 8

Cooking Time: 85 minutes

Ingredients:

- 4 sweet potatoes
- 1 tbsp olive oil
- ¼ cup milk
- 1 tsp salt
- 1 tsp black pepper
- ½ cup shredded mozzarella
- 4 bacon strips
- ½ cup grated cheddar

Instructions:

Preheat the oven at 400°F and line a baking tray with parchment paper.

Make holes on each potato, then place them on the baking sheet. Bake for 40-50 minutes, until soft.

Once cooled slightly, slice each potato in half lengthways and scoop out most of the flesh, but take care to leave a thin layer behind attached to the skin.

Reduce the temperature of the oven to 375°F.

Place the skins back onto the baking sheet, bottom up and drizzle the olive oil over the tops. Bake for a further 10 minutes to allow them to crisp up.

Add the milk, salt and pepper with the sweet potato flesh to a bowl and mash until smooth and creamy.

Dice the bacon and fry to your preference.

Once the skins are done, evenly distributed the mashed sweet potato between the skins. Top with the bacon, cheeses, and place back in the oven for 5-10 minutes, until the cheese has melted.

Sweet Potato Chocolate Mousse

Delicious desserts do often automatically qualify as unhealthy. However, with the sweet potato chocolate mousse, you can enjoy it without worry. The sweet potato eliminates the need for sugar additives, making it healthy. Make your cheating mud pie by outing this into a pre-made tart crust if you like or keep it healthy by serving with fresh berries.

Serving Size: 4

Cooking Time: 15 minutes

Ingredients:

- 3/4 cup pitted dates
- 2 cups sweet potato purée
- 2 tbsp coconut oil
- 3 tbsp flaxseed meal
- 1 tsp almond extract
- ¾ cup unsweetened almond milk
- ½ cup cocoa powder
- ½ tsp cinnamon

Instructions:

Soak the dates in lukewarm water for 10 minutes to soften.

Then, add the dates to a food processor and the sweet potato purée, coconut oil, flaxseed, almond extract, almond milk, cocoa powder, and cinnamon.

Purée until smooth and then refrigerate overnight before serving.

Sweet Potato Peanut Butter Brownies

This vegetable delicacy is healthy, dairy-free, and vegan perfect for desserts. What's more, the dessert comes gluten-free. What's more? If they can last that long, these are great as a mid-afternoon pick-me-up, served with some coconut yogurt and dried fruit and nuts.

Serving Size: 14

Cooking Time: 30 minutes

Ingredients:

- 1 cup peanut butter
- ¾ cup sweet potato purée
- 6 tbsp almond flour
- ¼ tsp salt
- 1½ tsp baking soda
- ⅔ cup white sugar
- ½ cup dark chocolate chips
- 1 tsp vanilla extract

Instructions:

Put the oven settings to preheat at 325°F and line a baking tray with parchment paper.

Heat the peanut butter in the microwave on in a pan over low heat until melted.

Whisk the melted peanut butter together with the sweet potato purée and vanilla extract.

Separately, stir together your baking soda, almond flour, sugar, chocolate chips, and a pinch of salt.

Combine the dry ingredients with the wet ones gradually, stirring well to make one smooth mixture.

Have the batter into your baking tray and bake for 20 minutes. The brownies may look a little underdone, but they firm up as they cool.

Sweet Potato Dessert Casserole

The classic fall-time dessert is a popular delicacy among Americans and one you will enjoy as well. It is sweet, warm, and homely, and a simple one to make. For a blend of cultures, get it while it's hot with some traditional English custard! Or a scoop of creamy vanilla ice cream will do just the trick as well.

Serving Size: 8

Cooking Time: 70 minutes

Ingredients:

- 48 oz. roughly chopped sweet potato
- Pinch of salt
- 1 cup brown sugar
- ½ cup shredded coconut
- ½ cup chopped pecans
- 3 eggs
- ⅓ cup almond milk
- 1 tsp vanilla extract
- ½ cup coconut oil

Instructions:

Add the chopped sweet potatoes to a large pot with some cold, salted water.

Bring the water to a boil, then simmer for 25 minutes.

Put the oven settings to preheat at 325°F.

Combine half of the brown sugar, the coconut, pecans, coconut oil, and a pinch of salt.

In another bowl, add the drained potatoes, remaining brown sugar, eggs, almond milk, and vanilla extract, mash together until smooth.

Spread the potato mix evenly in a casserole dish, and then sprinkle the pecan and coconut mixture on top.

Bake in the ready oven for 30 minutes until warmed through, and the top is browned.

Conclusion

Thank you for reading to the end. I hope that at this point, this cookbook has brought meaningful ideas your way when cooking sweet potatoes. I believe you have discovered that you can use many other ingredients and sweet potatoes to produce incredible meals. Sweet potatoes have various benefits apart from keeping you satiated for hours.

We have included 60 best sweet potato recipes in this cookbook, with clear ingredients that you can easily access. The instructions are clear for everyone.

What is left for you is creating time, getting into the kitchen, and making meals with sweet potatoes. It is simply a matter of time, and you will master all the recipes in this cookbook so that you can have different meal options for breakfast, lunch, dinner, or snacks.

All the best as you explore your kitchen skills with sweet potatoes!

About the Author

Since he was a child, Logan King enjoyed watching his mom cook. For him, it was even more fun than playing with his friends. That's how he fell in love with cooking. In fact, the first thing he ever cooked on his own was a cupcake, a surprise for his little sister, which not even his mom was expecting.

Now, supported by the whole family he is constantly sharing new recipes of his own creations. He finished a gastronomy academy when he was 18 and continued his career as a chef and recipe developer.

Now his goal is to educate and help people fell in love with cooking as he did. Actually, he is advising mothers and fathers to give their children an opportunity in the kitchen, because they never know, maybe their kid could be the next top chef.

Even though he pursued a career as a chef, his cookbooks are designed for everyone, with and without cooking experience. He even says, "even if you don't know where your knife is you will be able to do my recipes."

The gastronomy field is large and there is no end in the options, ingredient combinations, and cooking techniques. That's why he tries his best to keep his audience informed about the newest recipes, and even give them a chance to modify his recipes so that they can find a new one, one that they can call their own.

Appendices

I am not stopping with this book. There are going to a lot more so make sure you are ready for the amazing recipes that you will be able to get from me. You can always be sure that they are going to be simple and easy to follow.

But thank you for choosing my book. I know that you haven't made a mistake and you will realize that too, well, as soon as you start making the recipes.

Please do share your experience about the written as well as the practical part of this book. Leave feedback that will help me and other people, I'll greatly apricate this.

Thank you once more

Have a great adventure with my book

Yours Truly

Logan King

Printed in Great Britain
by Amazon

34512014R00084